USEFUL NOTHINGNESS

A WORKING
THEORY
OF
BEING

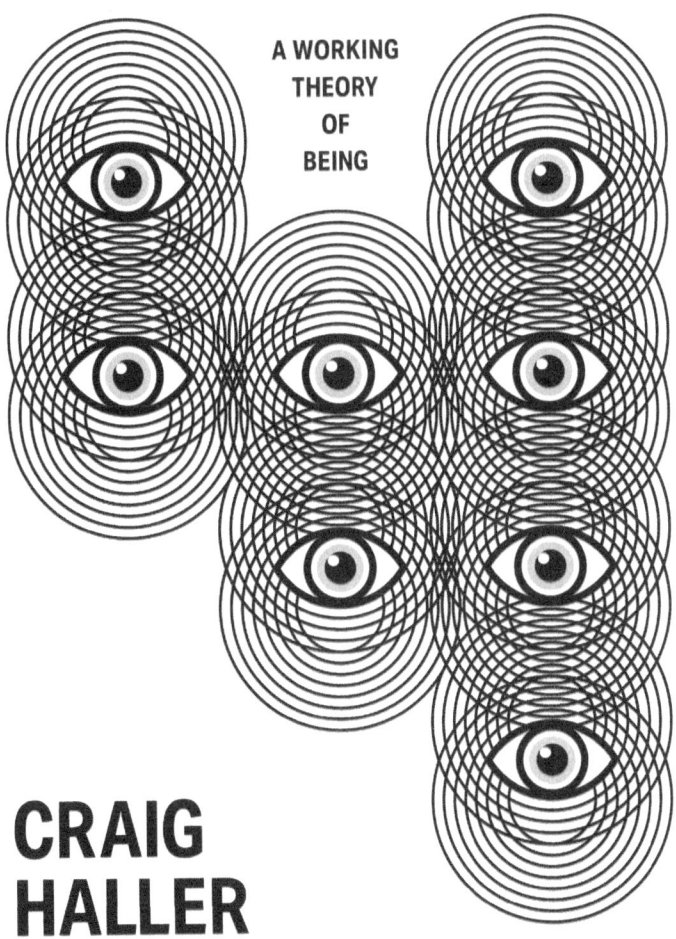

CRAIG HALLER

Useful Nothingness: A Working Theory of Being

This is a work of creative nonfiction, reflective prose, and poetry. Some names, places, and memories have been softened, reimagined, or veiled. Sometimes for rhythm, and sometimes out of reverence.

Art by Leanne Bridie
Published by Formless Editions (Nashville, TN)
Printed in the United States of America

First Edition, 2025
ISBN: 979-8-218-71435-2

For more information, visit craighaller.com.

For Nugget

"Being without being is blue."

— William H. Gass

PREAMBLE

This isn't a book of poems. Or essays. Or confessions.
It's an ambient archive.
A lyrical playground.
A bedtime story for the existentially curious.

If there's a grand statement here,
it evolves between the lines,
like a motif in a fugue,
returning not to explain, but for exposition.

There's no storyline to follow.
Only a rhythm moving quietly
between connection and collapse.

> *Let instinct speak.*
> *Let shapes reveal themselves.*

These aren't answers.
They're the sound of a question
when you're asleep at the wheel.

— Craig Haller, April 22, 2025

CONTENTS

00/ HOW TO READ A SIGNAL   1

    Notes On Form   3

    Prismatic Lens   4

01/ SAINTS, SUCKERS & SHAPESHIFTERS   7

1.1 Icons & Illusions   9

    Sisyphus Smiles   10

    Motel Bible   11

    The Devil Collects   12

1.2 Of Mercy & Mischief   13

    No Name / No Mercy   14

    The Ballad of Henrietta Red   16

    Sequim Cowboy   17

    The Bluesman, the Spy, and the Bugs   19

    Divine Bureaucracy   21

1.3 Delusions Made Flesh   23

    Sacred Summer   24

    The Reckoning Ritual   25

    The Unexpected Interruption (Christmas Eve, 1980)   26

02/ GHOSTS IN THE FEED   31

2.1 Simulated Selves   33

    Innervate   34

    Compassionate Nihilism   36

2.2 The Ache Between   39

    Abandon Preciousness   40

    Burning in Both Directions   42

2.3 The Programmed Voice   43

    Audience of One   44

The Grace of Getting It Wrong............................46

2.4 Coda, Etc.............................47

Dear Future, I'm Sorry............................48

Breathing in the Digital Age............................49

03/ THE QUIET INSIDE THE NOISE............................55

3.1 Soft Resistance............................57

Closure is a Lie............................58

Womb and Wake............................59

Something Unfamilial............................60

I Never Came Down............................62

3.2 Unsteady Truths............................63

I Once Was Pro-Lost............................64

Drift, Then Infinity............................66

A Comfortable Dark............................67

3.3 Interrogations............................69

Purgatory, Softly............................70

The Shape of the Question............................72

Changing the World is Hard............................74

Double Exposure (Refusal to Fade)............................76

3.4 What I Meant to Say............................81

Glass Logic............................82

Low and Away............................83

04/ INVENTED LIGHT............................85

4.1 Sketches Toward Shape............................87

The Sun Knows and Doesn't Care............................88

Instructions for the Formless............................90

No More Parachute............................93

The Broken Block............................95

Transistor............................96

The Playlist Question (in Threeish Halves)   98

A Silent Film (as told by an apple abusing itself gently)   102

Pineapple Pleasures (with apologies to boundaries)   104

Goodnight Brussels, 2010   106

4.2 The Shape That Stays   111

Blurred Memory—14B   112

Cloudform   114

Volume Control   117

Dungeness Spit   118

Unmoored (for a Dutch painter)   121

Three Dialogues: On Madness, Meaning & Making   123

4.3 The Light That Stays   129

None, All   130

Creative Split   131

Even Gods Laugh   133

The Seduction of Reason   134

In Defense of Defiance   135

05/ TENDER WRECKAGE   **137**

5.1 Fragments of What Was   139

Equinox   140

The Blooming Trap   141

Proof of Contact   144

Love Isn't Gone   145

Disasterpiece   146

Unintended Consequences   148

She Laughs in a Minor Key   149

5.2 When the Past Walks In   153

The Doghouse   154

A Man Appears (Breno, Italy)   156

The Laundry Room   157

In Bloom   159

The Gardener's Dilemma 162

5.3 The Reckoning With Self 165

Unfinished Wish 166

Glaciers 169

Every Note Betrays 170

Before Interpretation 171

The Edge of Everything 174

06/ THE LAST UNNAMED THING 175

6.1 Accepting the Deal 177

Benediction 178

Conversations with the Weeds 181

Echo//Ego 184

Drawn By Grace 187

Oak Tree In Reverse 190

6.2 Liminal Spaces 191

Non-Song for the Sea (Bar Harbor, ME) 192

Silent Admissions 193

Thinking of You 194

Waiting for God 196

Between Necessity and Indifference 197

A Cosmic Misunderstanding 198

6.3 Ephemera 199

The Jellyfish 200

The Soft Clock 201

The Chord Within Silence (after Rilke) 202

Clause Without Subject 203

Heaven in a Black Hole 205

Behold, the Universe 206

( ) 208

07/ FIELD NOTES

07/ FIELD NOTES   209

Afterword   211

Acknowledgments   212

About the Author   213

Praise for *Useful Nothingness*   214

00/ HOW TO READ A SIGNAL

Artifacts. Tonal disruptions.
Mostly poems. Sometimes prose.
Always listening.

//////////////////

Tone: Triptych invitation.
Theme: Drift, encounter, intuition.
Voice: Polyphonic, fugal, refracted.

//////////////////

> You're not here for resolution. You're here to reflect.

NOTES ON FORM

This work moves through fragments, dialogues, codas, recipes,
reports, myths, and quieter prose.
The forms aren't ornaments.
Each is an angle of being,
a container for creation.

Fragments crack thought open,
leaving room for what can't be finished.

Dialogues let voices press and overlap.
Unresolved, yet alive.

Recipes, reports, and transcripts borrow authority,
only to show how unstable it really is.

Myths and surreal tales stretch backward and outward,
reminding us that the fantastic and the ordinary are neighbors.

Lyrical prose carries the emotional arc,
holding the book in intimacy.

The structure resists totality.
Incompleteness is the point.
What slips the frame belongs to the reader's own archive.

PRISMATIC LENS

I.

Art forms a circle, a quiet aperture
inviting participation.

This book is unfinished without you.
It evolves in the space
between offering and return.

Read as you will.
Pause when needed.
Return often.

Meaning is made in motion.

II.

A tremor etches the page.
Something abrupt arrives.

Not to explain,
but to syncopate the heart's murmurs.

Not to disrupt,
but to reframe.

III.

Less narrative, more constellation.
Meaning emerges through
connection and interpretation.

Like a kaleidoscope,
each turn refracts something new—
mutations seeping through the lens.

There's no wrong way through,
only the way that finds you.

Every angle alters the view.

01/ SAINTS, SUCKERS & SHAPESHIFTERS

Memory warps into myth.
Strangers wear borrowed masks,
drifting through fractured tales
while the dust of old roads
clings to their bones.

/////////////////////

Tone: Mythic, archetypal.
Theme: Identity, projection, portrayal.
Voice: Blends folklore, noir, and existential theater.

/////////////////////

> We wear what was handed down and forget who handed it to us.

[1.1 ICONS & ILLUSIONS]

Some truths
wrap themselves in legend,
others hide behind a grin.

SISYPHUS SMILES

I searched for words
but choked on pride,
offering a ghost
when you wanted my hand.

Love abandoned
on a desert dune.

You asked the dust
to decide for you.
It answered with contempt.

I lifted hope,
you offered lies.

We drifted sideways,
unquenched,
chasing silence
at the cusp of Now
and Forever.

We bear our burdens
while Sisyphus smiles.

MOTEL BIBLE

Relapse lurks
like a motel Bible.

Secrets bound,
smudged by restless hands.

I opened it
to stir something holy.

A blurred verse,
or a guilty confession:

>   *"Tired sheets*
>   *shroud a shiver release.*
>   *They reel,*
>   *then collapse inward."*

A prophecy no one asked for.

THE DEVIL COLLECTS

Satan sits on the couch,
silent,
offering the mind ample time
to lose itself.

Memory fragments
blister and burst.

Panic.

The clock convulses,
quickening ticks 'n tocks
in reverse.

The devil revels,
stoic and still.

Floorboards crack open in slow motion,
spiraling down
to reveal a towering, rocky cliff.

The knees weaken,
the devil collects.

[1.2 OF MERCY & MISCHIEF]

They come from nowhere.

Rumored, feared, or misunderstood.

They never leave quietly.

NO NAME / NO MERCY

He blazed into town riding a roan mare
with a scar down its eye
and a prayer stitched into the saddlebag.

Nobody knew him.
But the wind rose when he passed.
And the dogs did not bark.

He drank in silence.

Smoke curled above the saloon lamp,
an omen postponed.
The whiskey did not soften him.

A woman with hair like fire touched his coat.
She said nothing.

He nodded once,
as if to mourn a future they wouldn't share.

At dusk he vanished westward,
but the sheriff's boy found three brass shells
by the river bend,
still warm with confession.

The sky pinked with guilt.
The preacher bolted the church doors.

Someone claimed he was an angel.
Another swore he was the devil.

Most just said
he was what comes
after mercy runs out.

THE BALLAD OF HENRIETTA RED

A beatnik woman named Henrietta Red,
    six feet tall with five-foot legs.
Hair like an onion, eyes like wind,
    talks in bebop, smells like sin.

Turn your back—she'll jack your car.
    Gin-soaked saint with an old guitar.
Riding the rails from town to town,
    stacking up dreams and burning 'em down.

Ink-stained suckers with crooked smiles,
    chasing ghosts through midnight miles.
Red-hot fire in the rearview mirror,
    a nighttime daydream filled with fear.

Beatnik preacher of the lost and found,
    switchblade tongue with a ten-ton frown.
Vanishing devils of delirium,
    a drifter's dream, a queen for none.

SEQUIM COWBOY

The cider foams, amber drift,
orchard mist condensed
at the rim of his glass.

Four-foot ropes of hair,
seaweed dredged from the shore,
draped across his western vest.
He leans back, boots cracked like old bones.

Over dinner, the names arrive:
blood-slick hymns of the Olympic dark,
serial ghosts etched in cedar rings.
He speaks of them plain,
as if describing rainfall,
as if a kill could be cataloged
like apple varieties.

I watch his lips move around legend,
the cowboy's jaw working
through marrow and cider pulp,
while the room tilts into some
makeshift theater of testimony.

Sequim blurs its edges,
sunset as punctuation,

coastline as confession,
his silhouette
swinging lantern arcs
across the small-town night.

Nothing here is ordinary:
  not the orchard,
  not the cider,
  not the violence carved into soil.

Only the way he laughs.

A low rope creaking against
the beams of a forgotten barn
pulls us back to the table,
where knives rest quiet beside plates,
and the sea wakes
beyond the glass.

THE BLUESMAN, THE SPY, AND THE BUGS

I was in a small nightclub
that smelled of stale beer and warm tubes.
Not packed, but buzzing.

The band was deep in a frenzy:
a swamp blues dirge pulsing with tremolo and sweat.

Guitars growling their secrets.
Drums pumping like a heart attack.

And the singer,
a middle-period Tom Waits,
howling from some furnace beneath the soul.

He was a prophet (or a warning).

At one point, he dropped to his knees,
pounding the stage with his fist
to the unholy rhythms,
as if trying to break the earth open,
or raise something up from below.

Behind him, a screen pulsed.
Not in rhythm, but in possession.
It seemed to know things the music withheld.

The camera zoomed in:

Tom Waits was now Bill Murray,
on an airplane, wearing a tux.
A double agent caught midflight.

Bill stared down the barrel of the camera
and winked, as if to say:
Of course I am.

The cabin erupted with faceless henchmen.
He took them apart with elbows and wit,
like James Bond on a bender.

Struck unexpectedly from behind,
he was expelled from the plane
and fell to the earth.

While falling, a voice began to narrate:

"Bill Murray fell gently
into a society of insects,
where he lived for several generations."

Fade to light.

(Awake)

DIVINE BUREAUCRACY

St. Peter presides at the pearly gates, calling court to session.

SAINT PETER:

>I critique the world
>and every last mess
>you made of it.

THE ACCUSED:

>Fine idea, Pete.
>But maybe
>we shouldn't be judged
>for flawed design.

SAINT PETER:

>*...go to Hell.*

[1.3 DELUSIONS MADE FLESH]

Repeat a lie long enough
and it forgets it was ever untrue.

SACRED SUMMER

sacred summer
the heat's too loud
star-crossed love
flushed with doubt

passion painted
on slatted walls
we sang as one
then watched it fall

vacant paths
forked the road
merge again
and then explode

sacred silence
beneath the lid
imagined words
we never said

what's up is down
what's left is right
we won the struggle
but lost the fight

THE RECKONING RITUAL

Dark feathers arouse suspicion
in the quilt-sewn night.
Placing pearls, like stars.

The gods intervene,
but only to record the damage.

The way inside
is guarded by conjecture,
like a small explosion
in a room half-asleep.

(even the moon refused your name)

I stood, destiny in hand,
and watched the shadows fall.

Alone at last:
        I count the splinters.
                I whisper their names.
                        I name them as gods.

I am aghast with fury.

THE UNEXPECTED INTERRUPTION

(Christmas Eve, 1980)

I. OH, FOGGY NIGHT

His festive shadow cast doubt on past glories.
"Why do good things get replaced by bad things?"
he muttered, sipping eggnog hotter than sense allowed.

The rearview mirror of his one-track mind
cracked beneath the pressure building in his sinuses since birth.
The eggnog wasn't helping.

(call it congestion if that helps you sleep)

You have to understand,
Tom was never a glass-half-full
or half-empty kind of guy.

He simply drained whatever glass was in front of him,
drowning feelings like wishful coins
tossed into a well of obsolescent obedience.

His head throbbed—
Christmas music blaring from the TV.

The cheerful tunes swelled,
stirring half-remembered promises
he'd already forgiven himself for breaking.

His jowls strained to crack a smile.
They nearly succeeded
but were interrupted
by a knock at the door.

"Who is it?" he snorted.

(no response)

"Goddamnit," he muttered,
in a reluctant return to bipedalism.

II. A GLIMMER OF REVELATION

At that moment,
he realized his life had not been wasted,
despite what his inner voices had long suggested.

He turned in a flash,
epiphany in hand,
when a second knock
shocked his revelation.

He waddled to the door,
exhaled an imprisoned breath,
and let the cold in.
Nothing could have prepared him
for the unlikely (albeit obvious) visitor.

It was Santa Claus,
but not as you picture him.

> *In this iteration,*
> *the gifting grifter is a 7-foot-tall penguin*
> *with a twisted goatee*
> *and a shotgun for an arm.*

Tom burst into tears,
ending a drought
that had lasted 39 years.

The weight of his worries
leapt from his weary bones.

Fear melted away
like butter in a hot pan.

He suddenly remembered the smell
of his Nana's French toast
as he fell back in his chair.

Santa strutted over
and sat on Tom's lap.
They locked eyes.

Something long overdue
passed between them.

They kissed deeply,
and began activities unsanctioned
by the ancient laws of the Pole.

III. NAUGHTY LIST, REVISED

Their hearts grew jolly.

Tom was rounding second base
when Mrs. Claus walked in,
appalled by the dorm-room display of affection.

Santa and Tom froze,
caught mid-reverie.

Mrs. Claus chastised them
for hoarding the sacred spirit of the season,
and for failing to extend an invitation.

She cracked wise
about the naughty list.
They all erupted into laughter
like a herd of tipsy reindeer.

Outside, the snow kept falling,
the eggnog boiled over...

none of them noticed.

02/ GHOSTS IN THE FEED

Scrolling through calamity
and calling it connection.
No wonder we're tired.

///////////////////

Tone: Digital fatigue, existential drift.
Theme: Attention, curation, selfhood in the age of anxiety.
Voice: Lyrical diagnostic. Melancholic. Speculative lament.

///////////////////

> You can't feel seen if you've never seen yourself.

[2.1 SIMULATED SELVES]

We create the mask,
then beg it
to recognize us.

INNERVATE

A fire
of thought and feeling
innervates,
a whisper swelling to a siren.

The whisper says:
>   *"Flee the blue glow*
>   *drilling through your skull,*
>   *draining your waking hours*
>   *with a sigh disguised as purpose."*

All is noise,
>   when I want silence.

All is fog,
>   when I want focus.

All is dream,
>   when I want rest.

All is fear,
>   when I want love.

Agency is a lonely ritual,
a mannequin rehearsing itself
in the dark.

Make friends with awareness,
but don't expect it
to return the favor.

Still scrolling
through quicksand hours.
A tide
of fear and loathing
floods the nerves.

Another whisper withered.

COMPASSIONATE NIHILISM

What breaks is not the world,
but the thinning veil of poise,
how we rehearse ache
in curated tones,
craving validation.

Sameness ensures safety,
but conflict buys attention.
Masks draw praise
when they crack for the crowd.
Gestures looping
like rituals in an empty church.

Entire lives spent
in borrowed faces,
smiling in mirrors that never fog,
blurring at the edges
until being
is performance.

A choir
complicit in its own undoing.
The mask fuses
to the skin, screaming.

We carry mirrors
and swear they're windows—
then wonder
why nothing watches back.

Fatigue honed to cut.
Compassionate nihilism—
the mercy of no longer pretending.

[2.2 THE ACHE BETWEEN]

Desire devours and delivers.
What you let go
might be the only thing that stays.

ABANDON PRECIOUSNESS

Cast it into the wilderness
like a plague victim
in a 19th-century mining town.

Leave it behind
like the cat my father
left on a rural road in '87.

Don't just wash your hands,
cut them off
and cauterize the stumps
to stop the spread.

Press a sword to its back and
push it off the plank
into the savage seas
of your subconscious.

Watch it sink
as deepwater beasts
dine and devour.

Preciousness is a lie—
your worth
made conditional.

To be precious is to be wanted,
but only until someone wants something else.

Break loose from sentimental cement boots,
or be served up as one last meal
before the deep.

Abandon preciousness—
it abandoned you.

Plucked from the womb,
trained to vanish
into labor, into debt,
into the metronomic march
of the subservient mass.

Abandon it
so you can meet
nameless dark
when the credits roll.

   Or refuse.

Either way, the sea takes you.
And it doesn't care what you clung to.

BURNING IN BOTH DIRECTIONS

The jilted sky poses a question:
Will you kindle hope?

Oh, useful nothingness,
flicker of light
in a darkened dream.

I am the match.
I am the wick.

I burn for what I love
and the pleasure
of its undoing.

Guard the light.
Greet the night.
Both belong to you.

Flicker.
   Fade.
Return.

[2.3 THE PROGRAMMED VOICE]

Say it loud enough
and even the simulation
starts to believe you.

AUDIENCE OF ONE

(a conversation on the erosion of urgency)

THE WITNESS:

> When did the search
>
> become the part you play?

THE PERFORMER:

> It began in a blaze,
>
> then a retreat.

THE WITNESS:

> So deception wasn't the point?

THE PERFORMER:

> No.
>
> I was only trying
>
> to fill a hole no one could see.

THE WITNESS:

> When did it stop giving back?

THE PERFORMER:

> When the pulse lost its surprise.
>
> Urgency bled out with it.

THE WITNESS:

    Does it move you now?

THE PERFORMER:

    Like wax fruit—

    shiny, tasteless,

    a skin of settled dust.

THE WITNESS:

    Then why hold it?

THE PERFORMER:

    Because I remember

    how it felt

    when it had to be said.

    Even if no one was listening.

THE GRACE OF GETTING IT WRONG

Such a joyous sound,
to be relieved
of needing to be right.

Create yourself,
let the rest dissolve
into laughter or wind.

No one's listening anyway.

But the wind remembers
every word
you never spoke.

[2.4 CODA, ETC.]

The individual isn't gone.
It's just under new management.

DEAR FUTURE, I'M SORRY

People of the future,

We were drowning in vanity, spectacle, and the rhythm of our own
destruction. I'm sorry for what passed as connection.

An inferno of mediocrity,
stoked by greed and borrowed rage.
Forgive us, if anyone's left to forgive.

`[filed in absence of better options]`

P.S. We danced in the ruins.

BREATHING IN THE DIGITAL AGE

Signal Report: HTI/OBSV-9

Classification: Human-Technology Interface Memo

Filed by: Observer 04–ΔΔ

Status: Signal intercepted in fragmented pulses

Condition: Persistent interference. Emotional latency detected.

//

ENTRY 1: HEAVY BOMBARDMENT (INITIAL PULSE)

In the beginning: comets, asteroids, uninvited debris.
Growing pains for a fledgling world.

Now, another bombardment—
not of rocks, but of information.
Unfiltered. Ceaseless. Indiscriminate.

> *"Billions of years later, I'm stitching half-formed thoughts*
> *and casting them into the current. A quiet offering*
> *to anyone listening."*

Observations:
- What once carved rivers now etches scroll paths.
- What once seeded life now fractures attention.

//

ENTRY 2: FAMILIAR GLARE

Symptom: Chronic curation.

Diagnosis: Untraceable fatigue.

> *"We suffocate in a vacuum of superficial distraction,*
> *reaching for connection in the glow that isolates."*

Condition noted:
It cradles. It cages.
We reach for it like fire
and flinch at the burn.

Protocol observed:
Reach → Flinch → Scroll → Repeat.

> *"We squander what is essential*
> *and are habitually overwhelmed*
> *by the great goddamn of it all."*

///

ENTRY 3: THE OPTIMIZATION LOOP

> *"Most mornings begin in a haze—*
> *thumb to screen before I'm fully conscious.*
> *I scroll through indifference*
> *before I check in with myself."*

Trend logged:

Update compulsion. Efficiency as virtue. Introspection as casualty.
Each improvement subtracts something unnamed.

Residual Humor (flagged for accuracy):

> *"I can't remember what I used to do while taking a shit.*
> *Just sit there and think? Like some kind of maniac?*
> *Maybe magazines."*

/ /

ENTRY 4: ALL LIGHTNING, NO THUNDER.

Stillness = deprecated protocol.
Distraction = default setting.

> *"Moments of waiting used to invite reflection.*
> *Now they demand distraction."*

Signal = Message = Noise.

If thought ≠ meme / soundbite → thought = erased.

> *"All lightning, no thunder."*

Result:

- Illumination without resonance.
- Understanding without depth.

"Time used to feel more transparent.
Now it's cloudy."

Still, a signal for hope persists.

"The dust will settle and we'll remember
what silence sounded like
before we forced it to dance."

//

ENTRY 5: HEAVY BOMBARDMENT (ECHO PULSE)

Theory:
Every generation believes its moment is the turning point.

Hope:
For silence as resistance,
quality over quantity.

Hypothesis:
If dust settles → memory stirs.
And with it → silence.
And the sound of thought.

//

CONCLUSION

- Signal persistent.
- Noise normalized.

Condition: Silence threatened, but extant.

///

Filed Under:

Cognitive Overload / Digital Anthropocene / Passive Resistance

03/ THE QUIET INSIDE THE NOISE

These are the soft reckonings we bury:
quiet yearnings, private fears,
and the unexpected peace
that finds us when nothing else does.

/////////////////////

Tone: Whispered revelation.
Theme: The personal, the buried, the refused.
Voice: Gentle, direct, interior.

/////////////////////

> The places you avoid remember you.

[3.1 SOFT RESISTANCE]

Not every rebellion
begins in fire.
Some begin with refusal.

CLOSURE IS A LIE

Old wounds rehearse themselves
then pretend they've healed.
Suffering can be summoned
with the lightest knock.

We limp forward,
mended, altered—
because closure is a lie.

We're the sum
of choice and chance,
outcomes we'd trade
to try again.

Life moves on without us.

WOMB AND WAKE

you began weightless
cradled
in amniotic dark

then delivered
into cold light

the same light
waits
at the end of the story

SOMETHING UNFAMILIAL

They were laughing,
not out of courtesy,
but because the past had cracked open—
like light pouring
through stained glass at dusk.

Something old.
Something shared.
An alternate timeline.

(broken glass, fused)

I watched from across the room,
holding yet another drink
that tasted like pretending.

I had never seen them like that,
not together, not tender.
It caught me off guard.

But I knew it wouldn't last,
that final flourish
of whatever reverence remained.

(aftermath of long division)

Their eyes caught a spark
as mine blinked back tears.

A glimpse of what I'd missed
and would never be offered twice.

Grateful.
Gutted.
Too late.

I NEVER CAME DOWN

Dim the glare
of your insufficiencies.
Move anyway.

The avenues that shaped me
were carved from the rock that rolls.

Rolling without aim,
an '85 Suburban carried me,
bumper-stickered from the inside,
every slogan and scribble
a slacker manifesto
meant only for those who rode along.

The air broke open,
rich with overtones,
a song too alive
to belong to anyone.

I was high
with nothing to do,
laughing at the miracle
of nothing to prove.

I never came down.

[3.2 UNSTEADY TRUTHS]

Honesty blinks—
hardest to see
when it finally arrives.

I ONCE WAS PRO-LOST

(after an imaginary conversation with James Tate)

I.

I once was pro-lost.
Wore a T-shirt that read
"Confusion Builds Bridges."
Held a punch card as a busboy.

Fell in love with Mary Jane,
who turned out to be a dreamcoat,
stitched from longing and steam.

II.

Now I'm pro-found.
I drink espresso and hum.
I sing like the closing credits
of a film no one saw.

But I know exactly
what the birds are saying,
flapping like atonal bricks.

III.

Now I'm pro-fessional.
Last week I gave a speech
to a room full of mannequins
on the existential weight of entitlement.

They clapped.
My god, they clapped.

DRIFT, THEN INFINITY

(A recipe for letting go gracefully)

INGREDIENTS:

1 cup fading beauty
¾ cup quiet yearning
2 tbsp soul fatigue
1 tsp ether (unlabeled)
1 tbsp unfinished business
½ tsp self-blame

2 cups scar tissue (coarse)
3 stiff joints
1 sprig of bitten lip
2 dashes of breathlessness
6 pinches of grace
1 tsp imagined closure (optional)

INSTRUCTIONS:

1. In a large bowl, whisk fading beauty and soul fatigue until softened.

2. Slowly add quiet yearning, stirring counterclockwise until vague.

3. Fold in ether and unfinished business. <u>Do not overmix</u>. Doubt will rise naturally.

4. Sprinkle in self-blame. Stir once. Set aside.

5. In a separate bowl, combine scar tissue, joints, and lip. Let it steep in memory (approx. 7–12 yrs).

6. Combine both bowls gently. If resistance appears, ignore.

7. Add dashes of breathlessness and pinches of grace.

8. Optional: fold in closure. (It will dissolve on its own.)

9. Let rest.

10. Yields: one quiet surrender.

TO SERVE:

- Hold loosely.

- Consume warm.

- Do not refrigerate what you're meant to release.

A COMFORTABLE DARK

We're not endlessly impressionable.
Things make sense
when we're ready to let them.

> *A mind at rest.*
> *A heart ajar.*

It's not that we can't see,
it's that we don't want to.

Reluctance is its own comfortable dark.

[3.3 INTERROGATIONS]

Every glance holds a mirror.
Every mirror holds a question.

PURGATORY, SOFTLY

THE MOUTH:

> The story was for my benefit.

> Alone in a reclining prison,
> something soft yet confining,
> stacked like chairs before closing.

> Purgatory is the star of this nightmare.
> I'm just in the crowd,
> watching it shine.

THE EAR:

> You assume I'm listening.

THE MOUTH:

> I search for words,
> but they splinter before spoken.
> Like a heart on stilts.

> I tinker with emotion,
> a radio transmission
> caught between stations.

THE EAR:

> Hope fizzles through the static,
> burying intonation.

70

THE MOUTH:

>Maybe God never offered salvation,
>
>a mere presence witnessing
>
>the pause between sentences.

THE EAR:

>Still, I give words to your fire.

THE SHAPE OF THE QUESTION

THE CHILD:

> Why?
> Why does anything happen,
> why does it hurt,
> why can't I know??

THE MYSTIC:

> "Why" is a toddler with sticky fingers.
> It tugs your sleeve and
> drips juice on the rug.

THE CHILD:

> I'd feel better if you just told me.

THE MYSTIC:

> You want attention, not answers.
> The truth doesn't tuck you in,
> it steals the blanket, hogs the pillow,
> and kicks in its sleep.

THE CHILD:

> Fine. Then what *should* I ask?

THE MYSTIC:

> That's better already!
> You're asking the *wrong sort of right* question.

Don't try to catch an answer,
it bites. Sit next to it. Let it mutter.

THE CHILD:

But I *still* want to know.

THE MYSTIC:

There's beauty in the veil,
and in not knowing
why the veil smells faintly of soup.

Some things are carved by chance,
others are sung into form,
and a few wobble forever.

You weren't given the riddle to solve,
only to watch it dance,
forget the steps,
and occasionally trip.

THE CHILD:

But why? I still want to know.

THE MYSTIC:

Because I said so!

CHANGING THE WORLD IS HARD

IDEALISM:

> They told me I could be anything,
>
> but I just wanted to be free.

RESIGNATION:

> Freedom takes the shape
>
> of the hands that hold it.

IDEALISM:

> I believed them. I had dreams.

RESIGNATION:

> Then you learned where the lines are—
>
> in classrooms, in culture,
>
> in social cues that teach you to shrink.

IDEALISM:

> But I *meant* it.
>
> I wanted to do something that mattered.

RESIGNATION:

> You still do.
>
> But ambition drowns memory.
>
> Checklists replace conviction.

IDEALISM:

It's not too late, is it?

RESIGNATION:

No, but you'll have to remember
why you cared in the first place.

IDEALISM:

I was a boy
who believed in change.

RESIGNATION:

And now?

IDEALISM:

Now I'm a man
just trying to remember.

DOUBLE EXPOSURE (REFUSAL TO FADE)

(A two-part study in self-erasure and seductive denial.)

I. THE MOST IMPORTANT NOTHING

Wistful nature recoils,
buried beneath a heap of hope.

Your opulent wings
have been idle too long.
Distant desires,
a trace of yearning—
allergic to satisfaction.

> *When did this happen?*

Bitter forces tether
what's meant to be weightless,
boundless,

until all that's left
is scaffolding:

an aging shell,
consumed by concerns
of the least-most importance.

Gone are the seasons
that carved this hollow.
Their bones lie buried in the roots,
and some part of me stayed there,
pressing a thumbprint into the bark.

But now is the time
to burn for the right reasons.
To rise. To fly.

You, always so eager to please,
must have been dreaming
when the moment didn't wait.

Creep from the shadows.
Face the sunlight.

And remember this (I should've said it sooner):
>It doesn't matter how you got here.
>It doesn't matter where you're going.

II. AFFECTION FOR LYING (OR BEAUTIFUL EXCUSES)

TEMPTATION:
>Affection for lying
>keeps you trying.
>Do you want the spark?

TRUTH:

> I know I shouldn't.
> But knowing means nothing
> without courage.

TEMPTATION:

> Then call it curiosity.
> A stranger knocks,
> offering adventure,
> promising the moon,
> and forgetting to mention the tide.

TRUTH:

> They promise escape,
> not peace.
> A window that slams the moment you lean out.

TEMPTATION:

> But the offer is elegant.
> Pride bends.
> Resistance softens.
>
> Fate feels
> like seduction, no?

TRUTH:

> The promises you make
> don't work anymore.

TEMPTATION:

> Maybe not.
> But I'll still reach the shore,
> soak it in,
>
> then slip back
> into the ocean
> that keeps
> your better self waiting.

[3.4 WHAT I MEANT TO SAY]

We spend years
writing the sentence
we wish we'd said out loud.

GLASS LOGIC

People notice something in me.
Quiet, disarming.

They seek validation
in the shapes that return.

> *The mirror I carry is clear.*
> *No smudge. No smear.*

Some see themselves as they are.
Others glimpse who they might become.

Some turn away, startled,
as if caught
wearing their own face.

Others stay,
softened by recognition,
willing to be seen without defense.

Acceptance isn't measured
by the world's demands,
but by what still glows
beneath it all.

LOW AND AWAY

The field half-empty,
a husk of hush and dust.
Chalk lines fray like old seams,
ghost geometry of games gone slack.
The umpire squats in his black uniform,
a priest of fatigue,
too tired to argue with the air.

I kept swinging at nothing.
Every pitch looked different,
though the arm was the same.

Writing's like that.
You miss more than you hit.
But the rare connection carries,
even if no one's in the stands.

Once, I fouled three in a row.
A kid behind the dugout chased them down.
He pocketed one,
tossed two back.
I wanted to tell him
those were my best sentences.
But you can't say that out loud.

Even when the ball dies in the dirt,
I swing, not for the scoreboard,
but for the crack that might arrive.

Language is suspect.
Every word a translation.
A curveball I know I shouldn't chase.
I swing anyway,
hoping one day the sound of contact
will be enough.

If anything here feels true,
it wasn't on purpose.
Keep it, if it lingers.
If not, forget it.

Even the abyss can blush.

04/ INVENTED LIGHT

There's an urge to make something,
even when nothing asks for it,
even when the ending feels final.

It's the trace we follow:
shapes emerging from the blur,
adored by what endures.

////////////////////

Tone: Generative.
Theme: Creation despite absence.
Voice: Hopeful, haunted, occasionally absurd.

////////////////////

> How do we respond when no one's asking?

[4.1 SKETCHES TOWARD SHAPE]

Sometimes
you build the form
to learn what doesn't belong.

THE SUN KNOWS AND DOESN'T CARE

Daydreams thread the evening air.
A hidden eye watches
without choosing sides.

Worn footprints trace the years,
but gratitude means letting go.

> *There is no me and you,*
> *only solitude in stereo.*

Relinquish the dream of clarity—
you lost the question long ago.
Comfort is another form of hunger.

Bury the keys in snow,
wait for the thaw,
then cast them into the sea
without looking back.

The sun knows your secrets
and doesn't care.
No quarrels. No qualms.
Only fire without favor.
A reactor smoldering in a sky
of endless ignition.

When the whistle blows
return to your work.
Tension passes
when you surrender to gravity.

Everything else,
a framework draped in your projections.
Not by family, faith, or fiction,
but by your own invention.

> *Do what you must.*
> *Then let it go.*

Redemption rises:
> not because you earned it,
> not because you deserve it,
> but because nothing else remains.

The sun, still burning,
doesn't flinch.

INSTRUCTIONS FOR THE FORMLESS

(Obscured Dialogue)

///

Transmission Source: Unknown
Channel Drift: ±0.7
Status: Incomplete

///

THE VOICE:

> You come seeking form?

THE LISTENER:

> I come seeking something.

THE VOICE:

> Leave your name at the gate.

[file crackles open]

> **ENTRY 1**
> The poet descends,
> not to shape,
> but to reverberate.

:: form is reverence, not requirement ::

THE LISTENER:

Is this meant to guide me?

THE VOICE:

No.

It's meant to unmoor you.

> **ENTRY 2**
> Bite the tongue,
> seal the mouth.
> Sing if you must,
> but only to the dark.

THE LISTENER:

And if the path dissolves?

THE VOICE:

Then begin again.

That *is* the path.

> **ENTRY 3**
> Fasten intention to an unknown tree.
> Leave no marks.

:: coordinates deleted ::

THE LISTENER:

What if someone finds what I've made?

THE VOICE:

    Let them.

    If it's true, it won't trace back to you.

[static builds; transmission frays]

        CODA (fragment)
        Oblivion is not absence,
        it's the quiet after meaning lets go.
        A cloud that wants to rain but can't.

THE LISTENER:

    Then what remains?

THE VOICE:

    Reception.

NO MORE PARACHUTE

(Aimless Invention)

THE ARTIST:

    At first, writing was an adventure.

    Drawn by mystery, anchored by necessity.

    Almost archaeological,

    an excavation

    of urges, longings

    preserved with minimal interference.

THE UNKNOWN:

    But what if interference *is* the art?

THE ARTIST:

    I'd rather see

    what the tide brings in

    than mark a spot on the map

    and watch the water pass it by.

THE UNKNOWN:

    No more targets, then.

    Only what rises.

THE ARTIST:

> Maybe someday I'll fall,
>
> entranced by shifting shadows,
>
> woven through cloudlight,
>
> with no promise
>
> of safety from the ground below.

THE BROKEN BLOCK

A broken block sits on a hill and waits.
It knows not why the hill was chosen,
only that it was once a part of something
meant to stand forever.

Wind erodes its edges,
each grain a question it can't answer.
Rain forgets its name,
grass rehearses its replacement.

Sometimes a bird lands on it,
and for a moment,
the block feels chosen again—
a brief empire of shadow and breath.

Then silence returns,
merciful and cruel,
like fate misusing a mouse.

Still, it enjoys what remains.

TRANSISTOR

The radio stutters.
The spirit jitters loose,
skating circuits that never close.

Number stations cough backwards,
choking songs mid-verse.
Digits fracture, loop, disintegrate.
A child's voice rattles coordinates
too fast to follow,
like nails scattering across tile.

A face with no mouth
presses against the glass.
Wearing glasses it doesn't need.
The giver watches,
eyes blank as stripped wire.

Smoke writhes on the shoreline,
not rising, not falling—
just flexing like it wants to leave.
The horizon tips sideways,
a coin that never lands.

Reception cracks.
Invisible waves twist in reverse.

Truth warbles, cathedral-shaped static,
a hymn collapsing on itself.

The lamp coughs light
into a room with no walls.
Maps curl in corners,
lines pointing nowhere,
compasses refusing north.

Footsteps stamp water
that has no shore.
Everything echoes wrong.
The listener burns cold.

The dial keeps turning
with no hand on it.
Every frequency a bruise,
every voice an error
broadcast at the wrong pitch.

The signal flickers.
Unfucked by expectations.
It keeps moving past the dial,
past the hand that built it,
past the need to make sense.

THE PLAYLIST QUESTION

(in Threeish Halves)

ACT I/II/III

In any case, my answer is this:

The playlist question staggered home
from an opium den in Tuscaloosa.

Took a wrong turn at a spork in the road and
ended up bussing tables at Tom's Diner—
mostly for jukebox access,
but also to earn bus fare
back to Wichita (of all places).

Roughed up, much later,
probably by bullies at a train station.

> *(PQ rode the rails*
> *the old-fashioned way:*
> *riskily.)*

Naturally, the train broke down
in a seedy neighborhood called QOTD.

98

Displaced, the playlist question
became a refugee of context.

Wrong place.
Wrong time.

And yet,
somewhere between scratch and hiss,
the question was answered.

A banger was born.

TRACK 8: AN HONEST MISTAKE

It wasn't supposed to make the record.
But the truth hides in the B-sides.

A field recording,
aged-out deep cut.
Hiss, breath,
harmonica oozing through denim.

The sequence was tight.
Clean transitions, rising arc, etc.

But Track 8 was wounded.

Half-dressed. Said nothing.

Nobody skipped it.

Nobody knew why.

TRACK 9: THE APOLOGY SONG (THAT DIDN'T WORK)

It opened with fingerpicked sincerity.

Soft ambience. Prepared piano.

The sonic equivalent of hands wringing.

Lyrically, it front-loaded remorse:

"I didn't know what I didn't know."
　　　　—a victim of recursive logic.

"I saw the glow, but not the fire."
　　　　—delicate, but dishonest.

Too self-aware. Too apologetic.

Like empathy performed at a community theater.

A guest verse came in:
　　　　someone from the old band,
　　　　autotuned from a time zone
　　　　no one remembers.

The bridge collapsed
under a metaphor
too heavy for itself—
it shouldn't have made the cut.

The song faded mid-thought.

A final whisper:

"This time, I mean it"
            —cut short by analog hiss.

Nobody replayed it.
Nobody deleted it either.

TRACK 10: FEATURING GOD (UNCREDITED)

She played tambourine.
You *felt* it.

A SILENT FILM

(as told by an apple abusing itself gently)

I bruise myself for company.
Roll slowly off the counter
just to hear the sound I make
when I land.

A silent film.
A metaphor.

I reach for the ceiling
but I'm on the floor.

My stem is a question mark,
no one answers.
I wrinkle toward wisdom,
though no one asked me to be wise.

Dodging rain
and passing planes.
The world flings motion
through my softening skin.

The city lights
magnify the haze,

but no one sees
a forbidden fruit
staging its own fall.

I hide the rot
beneath a sheen.
I invent new angles
to reflect the glow.

My sweetness turns sharp.
My memory:
cider and regret.

You call it spoilage.
I call it becoming.

Soon I'll slip
through the side of myself,
a silent rupture,
a soft collapse.

No applause.

Just a smudge on the floor
and a wasp who knows
what longing tastes like.

PINEAPPLE PLEASURES

(with apologies to boundaries)

I'm not easy to touch.
You'll need a blade, a plan,
and a tolerance for sweetness that stains.

Crowned like royalty,
spiked to protect,
I lounge on the counter,
pretending I'm not watching.

No one says, "I need a pineapple."
They just see me
and remember a vacation
that almost saved them.

My pleasure is inconvenient.
My scent: an invitation you pretend
not to accept.

I ripen deliberately,
bristled, golden, waiting.

You press in. I resist.
That's the dance.

The blade kisses my side.
I open slowly,
juices slipping like secrets
you're not ready to taste.

I smell like heat.
Like something remembered late at night
when your hand moves without planning.

You tear a wedge from my middle
and hold it to your lips.
The first bite is always too much,
too wet, too sweet, too real.

Now you're sticky.
Now you know.

I didn't ask for this.
I was content to ferment in solitude,
dripping poems into the air.

But pleasure, once revealed,
insists. It pools. It drips.

You call it overripe.
I call it honest.

GOODNIGHT BRUSSELS, 2010

I. CHECK-IN

She doesn't look up. Just hands me the key.
Her nametag says Chloé.
The edges of her accent flatten the vowels.
I ask nothing. She says less.
Elevator's broken. I take the stairs.
A sign says: *Travaux prévus prochainement.*

II. ROOM 219

Faint mildew. Heat that won't adjust.
Curtains drawn but still leaking grey daylight.
Rain clicks against the window like it's pacing.
I sit on the edge of the bed. Not tired, just waiting.
Everything here resists urgency.
There's no message. But I keep checking.

III. MIDDLE OF THE NIGHT (HAIKU)

Sleep came, then left me.
Box spring bed with burlap sheets.
First-world problems.

IV. LATE NIGHT SNACK

Three warm beers.
A half-eaten praline in gold foil.
The lamp flickers once.
I let it.

V. NEXT DOOR

Every wall here is thin.
A voice drifts through:
words I can't catch,
but the rhythm is intimate.
A laugh cuts off too fast.
A pause too long.
Then nothing.
I'm not alone. But I am.

VI. ICE MACHINE

Somewhere down the hall, it growls,
spits, groans, settles again.
A plastic bucket rattles.
Then footsteps. Then nothing.
The silence refills itself.

VII. THE COUPLE IN THE HALL

She's yelling—not loud, but sharp.

French. The words blur.

The rhythm is pure accusation.

He mutters in defense.

The key ring jingles like a threat.

Then nothing.

One pair of footsteps walks away.

The kind you don't chase.

VIII. SIGH OF RELIEF

The sign says: *Défense de fumer.*

I light the joint anyway.

The letters glare like they mean it.

I exhale toward the ceiling.

The smoke drifts through the warning.

IX. TELEVISION LIGHT

Muted news. French, maybe Dutch. No captions.

The glow spills onto the floor.

Every image wants attention.

None of them earn it.

I stop watching. The light keeps going.

It lands on my face like it knows me. I let it.

X. CHECK-OUT

Key on the counter.

She asks, *"Was everything okay?"*

The accent softens the edge of *"okay."*

I nod.

She nods.

We're both professionals.

No one asks what I was doing here.

[4.2 THE SHAPE THAT STAYS]

The truest things
outlive us.
They never ask
to be named.

BLURRED MEMORY—14B

Artifact Regarding the Unposed

THE VOYEUR:

> The subject and counterpart did not pose.
> The event appears unplanned.

THE OBJECT:

> You always begin with what I didn't do.

THE VOYEUR:

> Time was elongated.
> Motion resisted stasis.
>
> Your expression
> reached for something lost.

THE OBJECT:

> I wasn't reaching. I was remembering.
> Not reaching out,
> reaching in.

THE VOYEUR:

> You turned from the frame,
> a partial silhouette
> modulating memory under water.

THE OBJECT:

It was for my protection.

THE VOYEUR:

Silver halide processed emotion into an artifact.

Presence rendered as trace.

THE OBJECT:

You took a moment and made it still.

But that doesn't mean you understood it.

THE VOYEUR:

Every image is a failed containment,

but this one resists more than most.

THE OBJECT:

Maybe because I never asked to be held.

And you won't stop looking.

CLOUDFORM

It started as a stain in the sky, the kind you dismiss if you're not the kind who keeps looking.

I kept looking.

By the second day it had weight. Not heavy like a storm, more like a shape that refused to disperse.

The edges trembled. Colors slid sideways, like the spectrum forgot its order.

A bus driver swore it looked like a man kneeling.

The woman next to me said it looked like guilt.

I wanted to say nothing, but I said, "It looks like it's practicing being real."

No one laughed.

By the end of the week, people gathered in the field outside of town.

They spread picnic blankets. They took pictures.

The cloud didn't move. It thickened.

Sometimes it looked closer than the telephone wires, sometimes farther than the moon.

The cameras never agreed.

A preacher came. He raised his hands and called it a sign.

A kid threw a rock at it and the rock never came down.

A woman I'd never met touched my shoulder and whispered, "That's my father's profile."

Then she cried, though the shape was already changing.

I didn't want to believe in it, but it started believing in me.

Whenever I looked away, the air vibrated, faint but insistent, like a wire pulled too tight.

Not music. Pressure shaped into sound.

The kind that rearranges your blood a little.

I kept looking.

People tried naming it. The names fell apart.

People tried ignoring it. The ignoring frayed.

One man built a website cataloging every five minutes of its existence.

He stopped after three days, said it was starting to answer him.

The thing wasn't menace. It wasn't comfort either.

It was color that refused to stop expanding.

Standing beneath it was like facing a Rothko ten stories tall, only the canvas kept breathing and the red kept thickening until your body felt borrowed by paint.

On the fifteenth day, it rained.

Not water—something lighter, like the idea of rain trying itself out.

No one got wet, but afterward the ground smelled of stone.

The grass bent in directions that hadn't existed before.

For hours, everyone's shadows leaned the wrong way.

I waited for someone to declare it finished, but no one did.

That seemed to be the point.

It was neither arrival nor departure.

It was an atmosphere we'd stepped into, a room without walls, a

sentence too large to close.

People kept asking me what it meant.

I told them the truth:

I think it's holding itself together just enough to show us what falling

apart really looks like.

VOLUME CONTROL

The left channel runs hot.
The needle dancing red,
a vein about to burst.

Knobs sweat under my fingers,
warm metal, sharp ridges biting skin.
The amp growls like something caged.

Songs don't arrive. They bleed.
A bass line seeps into the drywall,
a voice leaks through the ventricles.

I keep painting it over,
layer after layer,
silence smeared like plaster
that never dries.

But underneath, it pushes back.
Every track ghosts the next,
each beat a scar that refuses polish.

It crackles, smolders,
burns through the filters
meant to keep it clean.
That is how it begins.

DUNGENESS SPIT

The morning was crisp, autumn sharp.
A wooden overlook showed us the Spit in all its glory,
tidal flats spread below, gulls cutting the horizon.
An eagle swooped by, huge and effortless,
its shadow sliding across the planks.
We leaned over a sign describing the terrain,
the geology, the native grasses,
the sort of information you always forget
by the time you reach the car.

That's when he arrived.
Blue windbreaker. Bucket hat.
Close enough that his presence pressed into our backs.
"Do you like to read?" he asked,
as if he had caught us in some secret habit.

We said yes. Of course we said yes.
He reached into a crumpled paper sack
and pulled out a paperback,
announced it was his "autobiography"
about his grandfather.
The sentence tangled in the air.
Autobiography of a grandfather.
A book about a man no one knew,
handed to strangers on a trail above the sea.

Then came the one-sheet,
creased and weary,
the kind of page that looked
like it had been returned more often than kept.
We nodded,
smiled the polite smile you use
when you're looking for an exit.

And just then, another couple appeared,
shell-colored jackets, fresh to the day.
We passed him to them like a baton,
grateful for the handoff.
They finished with him twice as fast as we did,
refusal made efficient.

Still, he trailed us.
Book in bag, bag in hand,
his intent trotting along at our heels.
The rest of the hike turned into evasion—
pausing too long at trail markers,
taking side paths,
pretending to study birds we couldn't name.
Every move was part of a choreography
to keep his pitch at bay.

Eventually the trees opened
and the beach stretched wide.

The eagle was gone,

but gulls wheeled in ordinary chorus.

We reached the water,

our hands empty,

our pockets light,

and the story of a stranger's grandfather

was not coming home with us.

Only the salt air,

and the quiet relief

of finishing a hike book-free.

UNMOORED (FOR A DUTCH PAINTER)

I stood in front of it for what felt like hours.
Blue on yellow,
smears of maybe.
Color bruised into beauty.

Unblushing light,
full of purpose
and spite.

Not storm, not ocean, not mood.
Just a tremble at the edge.

I stared,
transfixed by an ocean of indifference,
blinking stars fading
into dawn.

I made my peace,
but it was only a piece
of some incomplete puzzle.

Severed moments,
split by grief,
refracting a fraction
of truth.

I wanted to explain it.
Wanted it to be about something.
But maybe that's the problem,
this need for narrative.

Resist the illusion
of understanding.

No one reads anyway.

THREE DIALOGUES:

ON MADNESS, MEANING & MAKING

"The sleep of reason produces monsters."
– Francisco de Goya

I. MADNESS, BY DESIGN

THE SKEPTIC:

You romanticize it.

The vision, the unraveling.

As if madness is some secret badge of honor.

THE VISIONARY:

I'm drawn to those who live with conviction,

who follow the flame even when it scorches.

It still casts light; even if it draws monsters.

THE SKEPTIC:

You mean it casts shadows.

You call it clarity,

but maybe it's just delusion dressed up?

THE VISIONARY:

Maybe. But what if madness is a tax on vision?

A price paid by those who refuse to look away?

(impulsive pause)

> Let me be honest.
> I kept the wound open
> because I thought that's where the light got in.
>
> Let it bleed—call it beauty.
> Let it break—call it brave.

THE SKEPTIC:

> You're not describing depth.
> You're describing damage.

II. I AM FIGURATIVE?

THE LITERALIST:

> Explain yourself.
> Clearly, if you can.

THE METAPHOR:

> All I have are pretty words.
>
> Like a simile wearing yesterday's clothes,
> hungover and apologizing to no one.

THE LITERALIST:

> That's not an answer.

THE METAPHOR:

> I said something once.
>
> Someone said it meant something.
>
> So I said it again.

THE LITERALIST:

> What does that mean?

THE METAPHOR:

> Meaning's pliable. It shrugs into context.

THE LITERALIST:

> But context lies.

THE METAPHOR:

> Exactly. Like us.
>
> I smile like I mean it.
>
> I speak like I believe it.
>
> I stand like a sentence
>
> missing its preposition,
>
> or a star missing its light.

THE LITERALIST:

> You still don't get it.
>
> You're only a construct.

THE METAPHOR:

>If none of this is literal...
>
>then *I am figurative?*

THE LITERALIST:

>I stand corrected. Figuratively, of course.

III. SUFFERING AS CREATIVE ACT

THE VISIONARY:

>They only listened when I unraveled.
>
>So I stayed frayed. Attuned to pain
>
>to justify my anguish.
>
>They took the poem
>
>but left the night it came from.

THE SKEPTIC:

>You make it sound noble.
>
>Is suffering really the cost of beauty?

THE VISIONARY:

>No. Beauty is in spite of suffering.
>
>But fidelity to beauty,
>
>to meaning,
>
>is a kind of madness
>
>most people don't have
>
>the stamina for.

THE SKEPTIC:

And the ones we pity?

THE VISIONARY:

Maybe they're the only ones

who paid in full,

knowing the cost was everything.

[4.3 THE LIGHT THAT STAYS]

The line went dead
but the wire stayed warm.

NONE, ALL

Free me from the fetters of fate.
No top. No bottom.
No grief, denial, or hate.

Only love.
Acknowledgment.
Praise.

A harvest that starves the hand that gathers.
A mountain carried in a mouthful of dust.
Still water raging beneath the shore.

The river bends where it pleases,
carrying the sky with it,
catching the glint of a single stone
that doesn't move.

CREATIVE SPLIT

CONSCIOUS:

> I want the open road.
>
> The sun on my skin.
>
> To shape something polished—
>
> something perfect.

SUBCONSCIOUS:

> Perfection is a mirage.
>
> I live in fragments,
>
> in shadows,
>
> in stray impulses
>
> that resist shape.

CONSCIOUS:

> But there's joy in clarity.
>
> In control.
>
> In craft.

SUBCONSCIOUS:

> And truth in what seems dormant.
>
> In destroying perfection.
>
> In coloring outside the lines.

CONSCIOUS:

> Maybe we're not opposites.

SUBCONSCIOUS:

Maybe we're the current

and the wire...

IN UNISON:

A lightning rod,

ready for the next charge.

EVEN GODS LAUGH

Lanterns line the path of least resistance,
trailing light that sketches the face of eternity.

Each flame a dare,
a hush humming in glinting air.

Glancing blow
across enamored earth.
Dreams startle the soul's longing.

Laughter erupts,
bright enough to make even the god of no mercy
crack a smile.

> *What grace, to make a god flinch with joy.*
> *What luck, to catch eternity winking back.*

Between silence and surrender,
the light forgets to blink.

It simply remains.

THE SEDUCTION OF REASON

Art is the seduction of reason.
It bends the straight lines,
teaches them geometry.

Petals fall like snowflakes
beneath supplication.
Each one a small surrender.

Reason kneels before the inexplicable.
In the ensuing silence,
everything becomes beautiful
for no reason at all.

IN DEFENSE OF DEFIANCE

They tell you to keep it down.
Smooth the corners.
Say yes where no would be cleaner.

I've seen what comes of that.
A room where nothing happens.
Faces nodding until the nodding
becomes the only language left.

Defiance isn't wreckage.
It's interruption.
It's the laugh that slips out at the wrong time.
The note that doesn't belong
but changes the song.
The hand that won't stay folded in a lap.

They call it childish.
Selfish.
A waste of energy.

But every shift began as refusal.
Every invention began as disobedience.
Every open door was once a wall
someone refused to accept.

Defiance is a pulse that says
we're not finished.
The road bends here.
Try again.

Don't confuse it with rage.
Don't mistake it for hate.
It's the shape love takes
when it won't settle.
It's the insistence
that another world is waiting,
and someone has to start the walk.

05/ TENDER WRECKAGE

Shackled longings,
half-closed doors,
and names spoken into the dark,
hoping they'll answer back.

////////////////////

Tone: Intimate.
Theme: Love, grief, longing.
Voice: Unadorned. Wounded but still reaching.

////////////////////

> Not everything that leaves is lost.

[5.1 FRAGMENTS OF WHAT WAS]

It doesn't vanish.
It fades, floods, escapes—
hiding where
you didn't think to look.

EQUINOX

I leave footprints in the snow
each step a soft
undoing

silent powder
crunching beneath my boots
disturbing
autumn's hush

only a trail
of impressions and noise
remains

sudden joy

you were kindness
from the start
and I never
thanked you

THE BLOOMING TRAP

(with Ashes of August)

Building a forest made of flowers.
Not from need, but from a hunger
that stirs in the bone,
a longing that does not name itself
until the first petal opens.

They unfurl like whispered confessions,
each softer than the last,
aromas thick enough
to stop a siren mid-song.

The blooms rise taller than memory,
swallowing the sun
until the air turns liquid.

Fragrant kisses fall—
a honeyed rain that beads along the spine,
gathers in the hollow
where breath rests,
slips into the vein.

Their sweetness clings to everything:
tongue, fingertips, the back of the throat.

The aftertaste turns wanting into worship.

Apex bees circle in slow, drunken orbit,
wings tuned to the pitch of desire's ache—
something deeper, sacred, faintly cruel.

I try to leave,
but the vines have learned my shape.
The orchids pronounce it back to me,
syllable by syllable,
a psalm made of perfume.

They bind my ankles in velvet constraint,
like a lover too exquisite to resist,
too dangerous to trust.

Now I sleep beneath the foxglove,
dream in lavender tongues,
wake with pollen gritting my teeth,
still tasting the promise
I never had the strength to refuse.

Even sacred fires leave ash.
The garden smolders in memory's dusk—
seduction backlit by sunset,
wilted silhouettes asking not for forgiveness,
but for touch.

Seeking solace in heat
with no reason to burn.
Paint without brush.
Verse without song.
Beauty's ghost tracing the mouth of desire,
as passion falls endlessly—
only to land as ash still warm
against the skin.

PROOF OF CONTACT

We are reflections,
shards of light
and lament.

Every touch risks fracture,
yet still we reach—
drawn to the fault line
where ache becomes alive.

Pursuing
the gravity of longing
with unquenchable thirst.

I must have done
something right
to cross paths with you.

LOVE ISN'T GONE

Love isn't gone,
it's forgotten,
like a name
circling the edge of memory.

It knocks now and then,
soft and slow,
at a door
no one answers.

DISASTERPIECE

The plate slips from my hand.
It splits clean on the tile.
Coffee bleeds into the crack,
a halo spreading
like the floor had been waiting.

You shake your head,
but I can't stop looking.
The break curves like a river,
the halves still leaning toward each other,
even in parting.

The lamp still flickers
when I bend the cord.
The chair tilts,
paint chipped, cushion torn.
Every fucked up thing here
endures more honestly than I do.

Photographs blurred by unsteady hands.
Letters melted by the rain.
A guitar that won't hold tune
but still plays
when the heart is heavy.

We lived here,
clumsy, careless,
dropping, spilling,
loving each other
until even disaster broke into a smile.

UNINTENDED CONSEQUENCES

the unbridgeable void
becomes a compass pointing south

you follow it down
to see where it ends

it turns on you
plants your disappointments
in those you love

a concrete chariot
pulls you under
claims you as its own

the water closes
your hunger keeps breathing below

they'll wonder
where you've gone

SHE LAUGHS IN A MINOR KEY

She doesn't laugh the way the world expects, bright and harmless.
Her laugh slips downward like wine tracing the inside of a glass.
It carries something unfinished, a phrase that refuses cadence,
and maybe that's why I can't let it go.

It isn't sorrow, though sorrow brushes close,
as if waiting at the door.
It isn't joy either, though joy flickers there,
like a candle bending against its own flame.
It's the sound of knowing, of having seen too much,
and refusing to dress the truth in pretty clothes.

When she laughs the room changes.
The chatter thins, the air gathers.
People pause without knowing why.
Her laugh doesn't decorate, it inhabits.
It makes everything else look provisional,
like stage scenery about to be struck and carried off.

Sometimes I hear it in absence,
a phantom caught in another's breath,
a half-echo that doesn't belong to them.
It startles me, like catching her shadow
on a street she's never walked.

Her laugh colors the air as it passes.
It lingers like perfume on fabric,
impossible to wash out,
sweet and unsettling all at once.
The room feels borrowed after she leaves,
as if her sound is still choosing
whether or not to stay.

I love her for it.

For the way the sound dips and folds,
how it slides below the easy octave
where most people keep their laughter.
She won't ascend into the neat, ringing brightness
that others give away too cheaply.
Her laugh lingers instead, low and alive,
a song that stays under the skin,
a key that never resolves,
sweet with ache.

And yet there's danger in it too,
a thread that pulls me further than I meant to go,
that dares me to lose myself in her gravity.
It feels like stepping onto water
and finding the surface holds.

It's beautiful because it resists ending.
Because it curls back on itself,
carrying the ache of partings
inside the shimmer of delight.

I'd follow it anywhere.

And when it comes, when that minor music leaves her lips,
I feel it's meant for me alone.
As if the shadow in her joy recognizes the shadow in mine.
The laugh is hers, but it keeps me.
It takes residence in my chest,
a secret chord humming long after she's gone.

[5.2 WHEN THE PAST WALKS IN]

Some doors open
before you touch them.
Others
never fully close.

THE DOGHOUSE

Somewhere near Winnemucca.
January.
Mom killed the engine to rest.
After midnight, maybe, the gas line froze.

No one else on the road.
Cold enough to fear the worst.

A semi pulled over.
Two men inside.
Not threatening, exactly,
but the kind of help you don't feel good about needing.

My brothers and I climbed in the back.
The men patted the space between them.
The doghouse, they called it.
Mom took it.

Small talk. Awkward laughs.
Just enough to keep the air moving.

I don't remember their faces.
Or the smell of the cab.
Just her shoulders.
Stiff, turned inward.

She put us in that position,
and she was the one who had to sit in it.
Not out of strength,
but necessity.

We found a motel.
Breakfast in a desert diner.
Someone fixed the car.

The ordeal cost two days.
A bargain.

When I think back,
the memory's blotted.
Maybe repressed.

That might be when I first learned
how fear stays in the body.

We don't get over things.
We just learn to move around them.

A MAN APPEARS

(Breno, Italy)

Blistered silence, unasked noise.
Distraction dries the well.

A man appears.
His canes arrhythmically tapping
against worn cobblestone,
the sound uneven,
like rain starting, stopping.

A struggle toward destiny.
Each step a contest
between will and stone.

I rush the door
to ease his heavy burden.

The smell of bread escapes.
Church bells stagger through the square.

He lifts his eyes and smiles.
His gratitude breaks the language barrier.

I wish I could've done more.

THE LAUNDRY ROOM

The storm had been on the way for some time.
Not in a hurry.
It had other stops to make.

It visited my childhood home.
The wallpaper looked about the same as it always had,
though it had begun to curl at the seams in a way that suggested
it might one day pack up and leave.
The air was thick enough to chew.

The wind worried the corners of the house.
Something metal went skittering down the street.
It sounded important.

We crowded into the laundry room.
It was the only place that felt like it might
keep track of us.

There was a window where no window ought to be.
But there it was, clean as if it had been expecting company.

A towering black funnel ripped the sky,
bigger than the street, taller than reason.
It tore through the neighborhood,
rolling houses like dice.

It didn't take us,
though it could have.

We hunched together,
me, my mother, my brothers,
waiting for the house to decide one way or the other.

It rattled like a coffee can full of bolts,
but held its ground.

The dream let me watch.
Then showed me the exit.

IN BLOOM

I. MORNING GLARE

I woke this morning to the sun's orange glow slipping through a crack in the curtains, grazing my cheek like a ghost checking for a pulse.

Somewhere beyond the window, the faint sound of someone losing their mind ricocheted off the walls of my modestly decorated bedroom.

My eyes creaked open, dragging themselves through winter's hangover. I'd grown disillusioned with the world and the people in it, and wanted little to do with either.

II. DORIS INTERVENES

Months earlier, before this morning's noise, my half-hearted attempts at socialization had already been shoved along by my dusty old neighbor, Doris.

"You're a young man," she'd say. "The least you could do is act like it."

She set me up with a "pretty little thing" from her book club. Everything in me wanted to avoid it, but I've never been able to stand near a cliff without wondering how the rocks would feel.

Surprise, surprise: the evening ended in disaster.

Small talk? Poison.

People? Disappointing.

Her? Perfect.

Naturally, I said the wrong thing.

She punched me in the face.

It only made me want her more.

III. THE PACT

The next day, Doris told me I got what I deserved. I told her I hoped she got what she deserved.

She said my black eye matched my heart. Well played, Doris. We shared a shot of tequila and shook hands. She's alright.

The weeks blurred. Cannonball Adderley's *Somethin' Else* was on repeat. I couldn't get enough.

I was a caterpillar spinning a cocoon of jazz and isolation, waiting for the weather to split me open.

Winter wore me down. I needed something else.

IV. REVELATION

Back to that morning: the glow, the noise.

I staggered out of bed, parting a sea of red sheets, letting the spring light pour in like an ambulance I didn't entirely trust.

Outside, Doris was watering her daffodils, wearing nothing but what God gave her. Screaming words that didn't exist, pouring water over the blooms with the slow precision of someone giving last rites to the living.

It hit me like lightning: bare flesh and careful mercy, tangled together on the same patch of dying grass.

V. BLOOM

The scene cracked something open. I felt lighter than I had in months. I thought about going to her aid.

But I didn't.

We should all be so lucky to lose our minds in public and not care who sees.

Some never come back.

THE GARDENER'S DILEMMA

The tongue keeps tying itself into knots,
like it's trying to look busy,
like it's applying for a job no one posted.

Out back, the shame garden has taken over.
Everything in it leans toward secrecy.
Leaves huddle like gossipers,
the soil smells like it knows too much.

Seeds wait without moving.
They've gotten good at that.
They talk quietly among themselves about lunch—
whether it's soup today,
whether anyone remembered bread.

Once, a touch could lift them.
Now it's all weeds,
and the weeds know exactly what to do.
They grow with a confidence
that borders on arrogance,
their roots elbowing each other underground.

The rain arrives sideways,
then circles,
then asks if this is helping.

The weeds laugh.
"This is what we do," they say.
"You wanted growth. You didn't say whose."

The best flowers bloom where no one looks.
Maybe they like it that way—
folding their brilliance tight,
letting only the roots keep score.

Still, the roots keep feeling around,
as if something good is buried down there—
something they lost,
or maybe just imagined once.
They dig like detectives with no badge,
like undertakers practicing optimism,
like they believe the earth owes them answers.

[5.3 THE RECKONING WITH SELF]

Eventually,
the only room left to search
is the one you're already in.

UNFINISHED WISH

THE WISH:

       I still dream of you.

       Not the way it happened,

       but the way it might have been.

       The colors are warmer there.

       Even the shadows seem to agree.

THE WOUND:

       You left scorch marks where skin should be.

       I can still smell the burn if I think too hard.

THE WISH:

       I offered becoming.

       A place to rest your name.

       Purpose. Renunciation.

THE WOUND:

       And shame.

       You served it like a feast,

       course after course,

       sweet at first,

       then spoiled and heavy.

       By the end it was a dare to swallow.

THE WISH:

       I never meant to hurt you.

THE WOUND:

    You speak through broken doors.

    You always want the lock to turn

    but never the latch to open.

    Escape is just another game to you.

THE WISH:

    Forever was my promise.

THE WOUND:

    Until you woke.

    "Never" was the seam that split us,

    and you pulled until it came apart in your hands.

THE WISH:

    And still,

    I stitch what I can.

    I keep the needle ready.

THE WOUND:

    Stitches prove the injury,

    they don't heal it.

    They keep the two halves close enough

    to pretend they belong together.

THE WISH:

    Please, let me go.

    The weight is breaking me.

THE WOUND:

    I can't.

    You still glow when the night turns cold.

    You're the only warmth I trust.

THE WISH:

    Desire still brings me here,

    even when I promise myself it won't.

THE WOUND:

    I always take the fruit too soon.

    I should know better,

    but my hands move before my mind.

THE WISH:

    I want to be devoured.

    It's the only way I can disappear in peace.

    Some of me is already gone,

    and you're the only one who's noticed.

THE WOUND:

    There's less of you

    each time I remember.

GLACIERS

Signal Report: Emotional analysis, case file 117-B
Subjects: Love / Fear
Status: Dialog captured. Ambient temperature: sub-zero.

///

NOTES:

- Love offered joy, bundled with darkness
- Fear responded with clarity, bundled with contradiction
- Tension unresolved
- Observed pattern: bittersweet affection, cold sincerity, philosophical recursion
- Anomaly: peaceful admission of shared pain

///

EXCERPT (VERBATIM):

> *My love is bittersweet.*
> *My heart, filled with glaciers—*
> *drifting slowly toward their melt.*
> *What breaks is not the ice,*
> *but the things it buried.*

///

File under: Necessary Dualities

EVERY NOTE BETRAYS

The hard surfaces of the bathroom have no respect for decay.
They smear the sound of my voice, stretch it until it forgets me.
I listen to my own echo unlearn itself and return as something else—
a stranger humming through the tile.

Moved by reverberation, I search for words that might stay still,
but the only ones that come are already trembling into song.

To sing is to confess the lie of composure.
Every note betrays the wounds I tried to protect.

BEFORE INTERPRETATION

Five small reckonings

I. THE FORMLESS SHAPE

The watcher descends
without a map, only a hunch.
What's found is never what was sought.
It arrives half-formed, almost grinning.

Forget formulas—
impulse knows the way.
Say less than you mean,
mean more than you say.

Bury intent in tree rings.
Leave no map for the ones who follow.

II. THE LIGHT WE INHERIT

You began pure,
held like breath.

Then light
taught you to see.
It will come for you again.

III. CONDITIONS OF SEEING

We learn nothing
until we admit we don't know.

Facts knock
but never step inside.

Stories slip through the cracks.

Perception feeds on prettier lies.
Truth waits on blank canvas.

Stillness feels like fear.
We call it confusion
to avoid calling it clarity.

IV. BINARY COMFORTS

When nuance dies,
the heart runs to certainty—

black and white
to soothe the drift.

People once searched for love.
Now they search for likes.

V. THE COMA OF WANTING

An ego, mortally wounded,
bakes sunshine in the dark.

Dormant longing simmers,
its bubbles too shy to break.

It counts hours without a clock,
staring at closed doors
that never meant to open.

Sometimes a shadow sneaks across the room
with visions of rescue.

It never learns.

It only waits—
warming itself on the thought
of what it knows will never arrive.

And still, the night waits with me.
We don't speak.
Some things survive better in silence.

What we can't loosen, we carry.
What we can't carry, we become.

THE EDGE OF EVERYTHING

You'll want to create this feeling in others.
And you'll feel like a failure because you can't.

The people around you love you in their own way.
But they couldn't give what they were never given,
just as you won't receive what you won't allow.

> *Containment without reflection = stagnation*
> *Reflection without release = implosion*

So wage your war.
But let it be against the forces that bind you,
not the hands that would set you free.

Take up all the space you need.

A small room disciplines the mind,
but the open air is calling.

There is no tidy conclusion.

Only the wind in your lungs
and the names you still carry,
breathing in the dark
as you step past the last known place.

06/ THE LAST UNNAMED THING

Not quite an answer,
but no longer a question.

Meaning thins.
Names dissolve.

And whatever remains
has no obligation
to explain itself.

//////////////////

Tone: Dissolution.
Theme: Mortality, transformation, letting go.
Voice: Poetic, metaphysical, transcendent.

//////////////////

> The horizon won't lean closer. You have to walk toward it.

[6.1 ACCEPTING THE DEAL]

It ends not because you're ready,
but because every beginning
began as an ending.

BENEDICTION

This Was Part of the Deal

I. THE SHAPE OF FEAR

Fear visits in the night,
leaving quiet scars
and proof that nothing holds forever.

We arrive without a name,
and we leave the same way.

The world teaches us to live,
but almost nothing
about how to meet the end without clutching.

Perhaps the work is this:
to let love lead when we're weakest,
to let the mind grow still,
even when despair presses hardest.

Not to escape what's coming,
but to watch it arrive without resistance.

It was always going to end.
That's the agreement, silent but binding.

We're passengers,
passing familiar signs,
watching the road turn
into a landscape beyond memory.

We leave everything we've ever known
the moment our eyes close.
And we go alone,
but never unloved.
This, too, was part of the deal.

When fear is seen clearly, only love remains.
And so, for her, I offer this.

II. THE SHAPE OF LOVE

May she rest in forgiveness,
in strength,
in the deep peace
that is not given by time
but uncovered in stillness.

May the love she gave
rise like warm air,
spread across the earth and sky,
and return to meet her fully,
as if it had been circling her always.

May the fear in her body loosen
until it is no longer called fear—
only the quiet readiness
to walk through the open door.

Let her feel
the unshaken fullness of her light,
so there is no darkness left to hold.

If more years are given,
let them be rich with family,
with laughter,
with mornings that arrive gently.

And if children come after me,
may they know her
not only in memory,
but in the way her love
still moves through us.

CONVERSATIONS WITH THE WEEDS

ME:

There's a whole whirlwind of adventure under the storm.

You know—horses galloping, wind in the teeth.

I mean, I'm probably overselling it.

WEEDS:

You are.

Also, that's not the point.

ME:

Maybe.

It's our job to die.

To get on the good side of whatever made us.

Can't steer wrong

if you're not even holding the wheel.

WEEDS:

That's resignation in a bow tie,

waving politely at the executioner.

ME:

You strangle dreams under that stuttery sun,

and stand just outside my head,

humming a song I almost recognize

until I give up and hum it wrong.

WEEDS:

Still trying to figure it out?

ME:

Trying, sure.

But figuring it out's like chasing a ghost

that keeps tripping over itself.

You get close,

and then the worst thing sprouts,

smiling right in the middle of your nice, raked rows.

WEEDS:

And what's the worst thing?

ME:

Victory.

When you win,

beauty gets clipped, stuck in a vase,

and everybody stands around saying "isn't it lovely"

while it quietly ferments.

Trash night's Wednesday,

but the smell shows up Tuesday.

I've been living in that vase so long

I know the grain of the glass,

the way the light forgets my name by noon.

WEEDS:

>So walk away.
>We were here before your garden,
>and we'll be here after.

ME:

>Yeah, but doubt's got me in ankle shackles,
>sprouting moss,
>like I'm auditioning for "Statue in a Park, Act I."
>Running like that feels ridiculous.
>Hope's a delivery guy
>who switched routes years ago.

WEEDS:

>Maybe hope never promised the stop.

ME:

>My word is a loose screw.
>My intentions are bent nails
>that never held anything up for long.

WEEDS:

>Then do the thing.
>Or don't.
>Clock's still ticking—
>and the weeds keep listening.

ECHO//EGO

I said I.
It came back cheaper,
worn-out,
like it had been said too many times
by too many mouths.

I wrote it down.
The letters sagged,
tilted like they were tired
of standing in line.
I crossed them out.
The echo wrote them back in,
faint and crooked,
a whisper pressed into paper.

I closed the door.
The noise followed.
Sat in the next room,
pretended not to hear.
The echo dragged a chair across the floor,
loud on purpose.
Crossed its legs.
Waited.

I poured a drink.
The glass stayed full.
My throat stayed empty.
The echo coughed politely,
then drank from the air
like it had earned the right.

I tried for silence.
Got the hum of the fridge.
Tried for sleep.
Got the buzz,
the echo in the sheets beside me
shifting like it paid rent.
Tried for prayer.
The echo prayed louder,
to no one.
Tried for forgetting.
The echo remembered everything.

Around again.
Each turn smaller,
each step heavier.
Circling a drain long gone dry,
still convinced you might go under.

I walked outside.
The echo had already lit a cigarette.

Its smoke found my lungs.
I turned down the street.
The echo waited at the corner,
hands in its pockets,
kicking gravel at my feet.

In the end it was only me
sitting across from me.
Two of us,
nothing to say,
each waiting on the other
to make the first mistake.

The echo smiled like it knew.
The ego scowled like it didn't.
The pause stretched,
longer than either of us
could hold.
Silence, clearing its throat.

DRAWN BY GRACE

I was ascending a gentle path,
curving along a mountain
that watched the sea.

Evening arrived softly.
The light was orange,
like fruit still warm from the tree.

Lanterns lined the path,
not to guide but to comfort.
They hummed in the hush.

I was with others, though I didn't know them.
Their faces were peaceful and familiar,
as if we'd once carried water together
in some life before clocks.

We came to a clearing
and I drifted from the group.
I didn't want to leave.

Something unseen beckoned.
A second path,
lower, softer.

Drawn by gravity or grace,
I walked alone.
But I wasn't lonely.

The air held music,
not yet understood,
still arranging itself,
like joy rehearsing
how best to arrive.

And then a dock,
a gathering,
the sea opening its arms.

A band played
like they'd never learned a song,
only remembered it.
Voices rose around me,
not in performance,
not in striving,
but in one wide breathing togetherness.

People turned to one another,
embracing and swaying,
like the tide might do
if it suddenly sprouted arms.

And I felt it,
that rare unguarded welcome
that asks nothing in return,
that slips past thought
and goes straight to the marrow.

I stepped into it.
It stepped into me.

For a moment,
there was nothing outside of it.
No past.
No future.
Only the quiet fact
of being held.

A soft bell bloomed far away,
its tone folding into the sea,
into the music,
into me.

The sea kept holding me.
The music kept playing.

And then I woke,
still inside it.

OAK TREE IN REVERSE

The years don't run off,
they piss down your leg.

Dreams curl up
like cigarette smoke
in a bar that closed twenty years ago.

Regret's a busted jukebox,
still lit,
still humming the wrong song.

I keep waiting to grow into myself,
but the branches snap,
and all I get is splinters.

Truth is,
I'm scared of living.
And scared of dying.
So I drink my coffee,
watch the dust float,
each speck hanging in its own light,
and let the day pass through me.

[6.2 LIMINAL SPACES]

You're not lost,
you're dissolving.
Softening at the edges
where certainty used to live,
and the unknown waits patiently.
A low sky, a slow breath, and no map.

NON-SONG FOR THE SEA

(Bar Harbor, ME)

I fixate on rock and tide.
An eternity of ocean
articulates
with hypnotic force.

A scrappy gull chorus
hunts the shoreline,
cracking mollusks
on wet stone.

They satiate the day.

Waves break like thunder,
leaving behind a fizzy fog
that scatters beyond
the span of my affection.

I say how small we must be.

The ocean says nothing—
just keeps rocking
back and forth.

SILENT ADMISSIONS

I open my mouth,
the words collapse.

What I mean shrinks
the moment it's spoken.

So I hold it,
let the silence thicken,
let it do the work
I can't.

But silence grows teeth.
It exaggerates.
It drags the unsaid
into the open,
heavier than any sentence.

Between us
nothing was said.
Between us
everything was.

THINKING OF YOU

I got a card today.
It said: *Thinking of You.*

I held it for a while,
feeling the grain of the paper.
Wondering how far those words traveled
before they landed here.

You're not here to read it,
but if you were,
I'd probably just hand you the card
and let it speak for itself.

Lately, I've been thinking of you
the way seasons think of the trees.
Not as something to keep,
but as something they circle back to,
aware the shape will change
every time they meet again.

The card's still on the table.

It doesn't ask for anything.
It just sits there,
holding a thought in place

the way a kettle holds heat
after the flame's gone out.

And I realize:
thinking isn't knowing,
knowing isn't holding,
and holding's not the same as having.

Sometimes the kindest thing
is to set it down
and let it cool.

WAITING FOR GOD

A man sits on the curb
with a paper cup.
He says he's waiting for God
to fill it.

The cup has a crack.
The crack is spreading.

Cars cough.
Horns bark.
Nobody stops.

The cup stays empty.
So does the man.

Stillness doesn't answer,
it reflects.

      (that counts as something)

Maybe you don't find God.
      Maybe you just wait.
          Maybe you stop.

Maybe you just stop needing to.

BETWEEN NECESSITY AND INDIFFERENCE

At the bus stop, Necessity wore a raincoat two sizes too big.
Indifference leaned against the pole eating sunflower seeds.
Desire showed up late carrying a broken umbrella.
Hesitation was already there but pretended not to notice.

Someone said the bus was coming.
Someone else said there was never a bus.
Everyone agreed to wait.

A pigeon strutted in circles,
dragging a receipt from the grocery store.
We watched it like it had the answer.

When the bus finally arrived, no one got on.
We were too busy arguing about who had been hiding
and whether the game had already ended.

A COSMIC MISUNDERSTANDING

I look into the darkness
and it looks back.
Not with menace,
but with patience.

The stars are small voices,
each carrying a question
older than speech.

We argue right and wrong
like children tracing lines in the dust,
while galaxies wheel overhead
with no thought of sides.

Life leans toward me,
half-smile, half-silence.

I reach—
and the reaching itself
becomes the answer.

[6.3 EPHEMERA]

Whatever couldn't stay
in one place ends here.

THE JELLYFISH

translucent wash
you burn me every time
forget the rules

no
forget yourself instead

your spine is cracked
your knuckles scraped

a burden
to remember

THE SOFT CLOCK

The clock grows soft in my hands.
Its numbers drip into the sand,
still ticking as they sink.

A fish gasps on the windowsill.
The curtains breathe like lungs.
The floor tilts toward an unseen sea.

I try to hold my shape,
but my shadow bends,
peeling from the wall
like wet paper.

Expansion isn't progress,
it's the body melting
into a form it never chose,
the mind stretching
until thought hangs slack,
a face in the mirror
longer than memory.

To expand beyond yourself
is to watch the self slide off the table.

There is no sound.

THE CHORD WITHIN SILENCE

(after Rilke)

Compassion moves across me
like a soft hand
over an old wound.

I retreat without haste,
settling into the corners of the room.

Silence stirs again, subtle now,
clever in the ways it hides its weight.

Regret ripens within reach,
a gilded fruit I will not taste.
Its sweetness unravels me.

Today there is no instrument,
only the chord
that swells inside the stillness.

Sounds return dressed
in the colors of other Things,
and somewhere unseen strings
tremble with shapes and names
I never learned to say.

CLAUSE WITHOUT SUBJECT

(with apologies to Wittgenstein)

Whereof the self presumed to speak,
the structure collapsed.

Whereof the structure held,
no self could be found.

I attempted "I"
as though the word
could fasten me in place.

But each shape bent back—
a sentence circling
its own echo.

The seeing was never a seeing-of.
The self, never subject,
only verb.
Only clause.

A mirror. A window.
I tried to tell the difference.
I don't anymore.

The gesture only gestures.
Something almost occurs,
then withdraws.

Not visibility.
Not salvation.
Only the trace
of wanting either.

Whereof one cannot speak,
there, too, is the self.

HEAVEN IN A BLACK HOLE

Heaven in a black hole,
a singularity waiting,
stretched beyond itself
until it becomes
everything.

The heart does this too,
folding on its ache
until it bursts.

Maybe something
will find it useful.

BEHOLD, THE UNIVERSE

Dust gathers slowly
in the indifferent dark.

A thunderous voice
tears open the void,
summoning rhythm
from silence,
fire from nothing.

Primordial forces
clash and converge,
then settle into tones
too vast to name,
serene only in their magnitude.

Eternity unspools—
layer after layer,
each heavier than breath,
each asking to be borne.

Mystery leans in,
not gentle but absolute.

Listening with an ear
that devours sound,

the stars convene
like conspirators,
a glimmering hush
charged with intent.

Stardust cascades,
not falling but flooding,
dissolving into breath,
into bone,
into every porous surface.

Defenses collapse.
Euphoria unhinged.

( )

If this were the end,
would you know it?

Or would you keep
reading outside
the frame?

07/ FIELD NOTES

What remains after the offering.
Gratitude. Glimpses.
And a name.

//////////////////

Tone: Retrospective, clarifying, grateful
Theme: Legacy, influence, identity
Voice: Personal, humble, archival

//////////////////

> You won't find closure. Just fingerprints.

AFTERWORD

Music shaped how I write. It taught me to listen to rhythm, to tone, to silence. To step aside. To let a single line carry what it can.

This didn't begin as a book. Just loose pages, pocket notebooks, poems in margins of my favorite books. Lines arriving in bursts, in hotel rooms, on planes, in dreams.

I kept molding what felt alive until a shape began to gather. Different forms and voices appeared without warning. Some evolved. Others vanished as quickly as they came.

There's no clean ending to work like this. The pieces don't close; they keep moving, even when I'm no longer following.

What happens next is yours.

Nothing here is finished. But I've taken it as far as I can. I have music to make.

ACKNOWLEDGMENTS

I don't know where my voice ends and yours begins.

Somewhere between Rilke and James Tate.
Between Jeff Tweedy and Henry Miller.
Between the way Bukowski ignored punctuation
and the way Josh Ritter doesn't.

Tom Waits turned a junkyard into a temple for the downtrodden.
Coltrane found God through music.
Brian Wilson built a cathedral of ache and left the door wide open.
Radiohead showed me how to haunt something gently.

The *Tao Te Ching* gave me breath.
Krishnamurti shattered my fragile notions.
Kierkegaard sharpened doubt like a knife.
Barthelme taught absurdity to sing.

Bosch sketched the blueprints for madness.
Dalí painted dreams that refuse to explain themselves.
Rothko made stillness burn.

I owe something to each of them.

You're here, too.

ABOUT THE AUTHOR

Craig Haller is a writer, musician, and observer of stray moments.

Useful Nothingness is his first book. It's an assemblage of fragments and tensions, shaped by what resists explanation but insists on being felt. His work drifts between clarity and contradiction, grounded in a lifetime of songwriting and a trust in what intuition reveals.

He lives in Nashville, where he records music, collects impressions, and tries to stay inspired long enough to write down what the silence says.

Visit craighaller.com.

PRAISE FOR *USEFUL NOTHINGNESS*

"If Søren Kierkegaard and a lo-fi cassette tape had a child, and that child grew up in a library of fog, this would be its diary."
   – Notional Geographic

"It undresses slowly. Not to seduce, but to bleed a little on the floor."
   – Big Sur, Little Sur

"For anyone who has ever stared at a ceiling and wondered what it means to be a 'self'—this book is for you. And also for the ceiling."
   – Cognitive Drift Almanac

"I was 32% more emotionally available after reading it, according to my ex."
   – Sentiment Analysis Monthly

"A literary Meow Wolf—immersive, full of secrets. Like a hushed exhibit in a high-desert cathedral."
   – 505 Letters

"A work of spiritual resonance disguised as ambient literature. It is not therapeutic, but it is healing. It offers no answers, but opens the aperture for better questions."
   – What You Should've Said

"Best read at night, under quiet duress."
   – The Inevitable Review

"It's not often we receive a manuscript and whisper to it, 'Thank you for not trying to fix me.' This is that kind of book."
   – The Occasionalist

"An ambient museum of spiritual misfires, memory fractures, and refracted selves."
   – Dave

"Useful Nothingness doesn't beg for your attention. It just sits in the room with you, quietly breaking your heart."
   – An Old Acquaintance

"This book does not aim to teach or resolve. It asks questions with such patience and odd warmth that the absence of answers becomes a kind of answer itself."
   – The Subterranean Renaissance